HAUNTED
WORLD

FAMOUS
GHOST STO
OF NORTH
AMERICA

by Matt Chandler

CAPSTONE PRESS
a capstone imprint

Edge Books are published by Capstone Press,
1710 Roe Crest Drive, North Mankato, Minnesota 56003
www.mycapstone.com

Library of Congress Cataloging-in-Publication Data
Library of Congress Cataloging-in-Publication Data is available on the Library
of Congress website.
ISBN: 978-1-5435-2595-3 (hardcover)
ISBN: 978-1-5435-2599-1 (paperback)
ISBN: 978-1-5435-2603-5 (eBook PDF)

Editorial Credits
Carrie Braulick Sheely, editor; Kyle Grenz, designer; Svetlana Zhurkin,
media researcher; Kathy McColley, production specialist

Photo Credits
Alamy: Karina Tkach, 24–25; AP Images: Dylan Lovan, 7, Patron Spirits/
Greg Wahl-Stephens, 15; Courtesy of the Federal Bureau of Investigations,
27; Dreamstime: Jackbluee, 8, Ruud Glasbergen, cover (back left), 11; Getty
Images: UIG/Wild Horizons, 18–19; iStockphoto: Spanglish, cover (back right),
10; Library of Congress, 26–27; Matt Chandler, 20; Newscom: Danita Delimont
Photography/Walter Bibikow, 16; North Wind Picture Archives, 12; Shutterstock:
Ad_hominem (map), 5, 8, 10, 12, 14, 16, 18, 20, 22, 24, 26, 29, Amir Bajrich, 6,
Benny Marty, 28, Chepe Nicoli, 17, chloe7992, 21, Joe Prachatree, cover (front),
Marcos Carvalho, 13, MartinMojzis, 23, MM Stock, 5, photo.ua, 14, windsketch, 4

Design Elements by Shutterstock

Printed and bound in the USA.
PA017

TABLE OF CONTENTS

Spooky Sights in North America

People tell spooky ghost stories in every corner of the world. Stories about North America's **haunted** places are just as varied as the continent's landscape. Are armed ghosts fighting military battles that ended hundreds of years ago? Do ghosts of children haunt a Mexican museum filled with mummies? Could the headless ghost of a train conductor be looking for his head in Canada's countryside? Explore some of the scariest ghost tales of North America and decide for yourself.

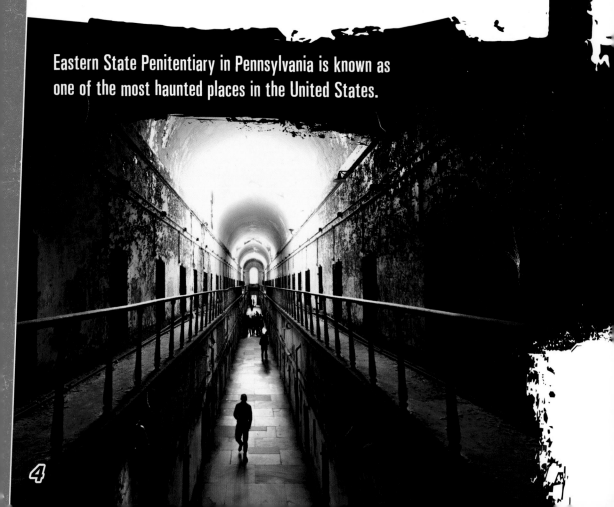

Eastern State Penitentiary in Pennsylvania is known as one of the most haunted places in the United States.

Waverly Hills Sanatorium

LOCATION: LOUISVILLE, KENTUCKY

In 1910 a small hospital opened in Louisville, Kentucky, to treat people suffering from **tuberculosis**. There was no cure for the disease. As the disease spread, a larger hospital opened on the site called Waverly Hills Sanatorium. Before Waverly Hills closed in 1961, as many as 6,000 people had died there. Today it is said to be one of the most haunted places in the United States.

FACT

The doctors at Waverly Hills didn't want patients to see the dead bodies being carried out. Workers built a tunnel to move the bodies out of the hospital. The tunnel became known as the "Death Chute."

haunted—having mysterious events happen often, possibly due to visits from ghosts

tuberculosis—a disease caused by bacteria that causes fever, weight loss, and coughing; left untreated, tuberculosis can lead to death

5

The ghost of a young boy named Timmy is one of the most famous ghosts at Waverly Hills. When Timmy was a patient at Waverly, it's said he loved to play with a leather ball. After hearing this story, hospital visitors began bringing brightly colored balls for him. Some visitors say they have placed balls on the ground and asked Timmy to play. The balls then rolled across the floor without being touched.

People have reported seeing the ghosts of former patients throughout the hospital. They include the ghost of an elderly woman who roams the hospital bleeding from her chained hands and feet. A dark shadowy ghost called the Creeper is said to bring a feeling of doom to anyone who is nearby.

Room 502 is considered one of the most haunted places in the hospital. Stories say a nurse took her own life there. People have reported seeing a ghostly uniformed nurse in the room. Some witnesses said she told them to get out. In 2010 a team of ghost hunters investigated the hospital for their TV show. They claim to have recorded ghostly voices in the room.

FACT

Many people have reported smelling food cooking in the kitchen at Waverly Hills. But the kitchen has been shut down for years!

Waverly Hills has been empty since 1981. But it remains a popular attraction for ghost hunters and other tourists.

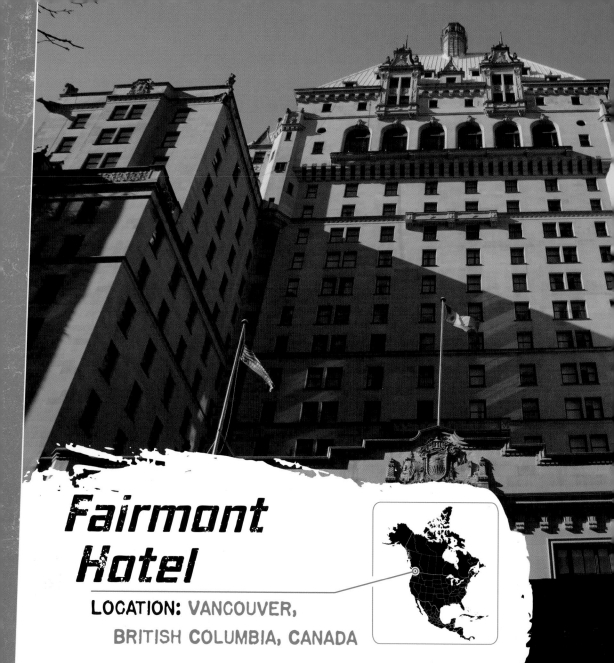

Fairmont Hotel

LOCATION: VANCOUVER, BRITISH COLUMBIA, CANADA

From the outside, the Fairmont Hotel appears to be just another luxury hotel in Vancouver. But it may not be as commonplace as it seems. Some visitors have left the building convinced it's haunted.

The most famous ghost story tells of a woman named Jennie Pearl Cox. She often visited the Fairmont Hotel to attend social events in the early 1940s. Cox was killed in a car accident in front of the hotel. Since then, visitors have reported seeing the ghost of a beautiful woman dressed in a red gown wandering the hotel. The ghost often walks through elevator doors. The "Lady in Red" stays mostly on the 14th floor. Some 14th-floor guests have said the Lady in Red was in their rooms.

In 2017 a man snapped a photo he said proved the Lady in Red was haunting the Fairmont. The image appears to show a figure in red staring out a 14th-floor window. When the photo was taken, the 14th floor was closed to guests while repairs were being made. **Skeptics** say it might have been a red tarp or other piece of material that repair workers placed there.

skeptic—a person who questions things that other people believe in

Island of the Dolls

For many children, dolls are a source of happiness and comfort. But quite the opposite is true if the dolls are eyeless, limbless objects filled with evil **spirits**. A small island near Mexico City is said to be haunted by the ghost of a young girl who drowned nearby. According to a **legend**, Julian Santana Barrera found the girl dead in the water. He also found a doll floating in the water near her body. He hung the doll from a nearby tree to honor the young girl. But he soon heard unexplained screams and footsteps. He believed the ghost of the girl haunted the area. He then began to collect hundreds of dolls, hanging them from trees all over the island. He believed they would make her ghost happy. Today more than 1,000 dolls fill the island. Many of them are falling apart and have missing eyes or limbs. Their ragged appearance only adds to the creepiness of the island.

spirit—the invisible part of a person that contains thoughts and feelings; some people believe the spirit leaves the body after death

legend—a story passed down through the years that may not be completely true

Visitors to the "Island of the Dolls" report several **paranormal** experiences. Some people have reported the dolls whispering to them. Others have claimed the eyes in the dolls have moved as if watching them. The experiences have led some people to believe the dolls are **possessed** by the dead girl's ghost.

Barrera died in 2001. Since then more people have visited the island. Many of them hang up their own dolls on trees. Some of these visitors continue to report paranormal events.

paranormal—having to do with an event that
    has no scientific explanation

possessed—to be controlled by an evil spirit

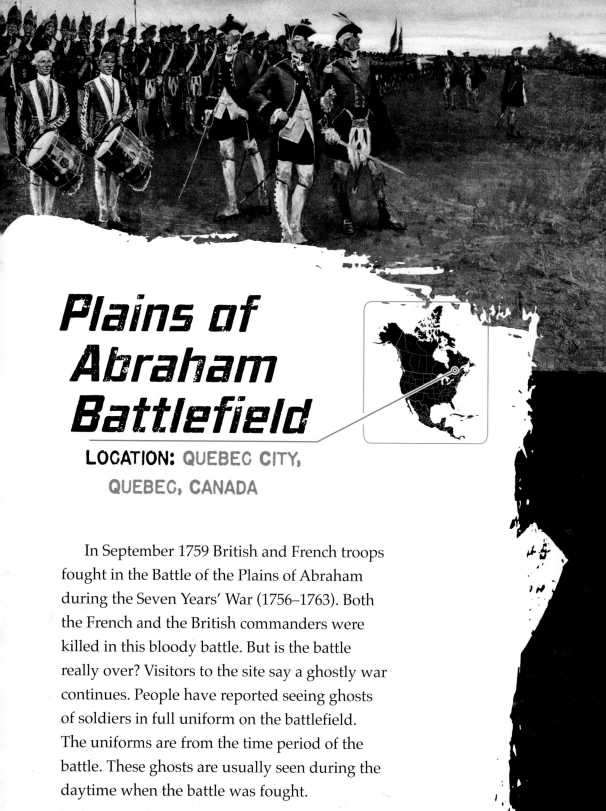

Plains of Abraham Battlefield

LOCATION: QUEBEC CITY, QUEBEC, CANADA

In September 1759 British and French troops fought in the Battle of the Plains of Abraham during the Seven Years' War (1756–1763). Both the French and the British commanders were killed in this bloody battle. But is the battle really over? Visitors to the site say a ghostly war continues. People have reported seeing ghosts of soldiers in full uniform on the battlefield. The uniforms are from the time period of the battle. These ghosts are usually seen during the daytime when the battle was fought.

A series of tunnels is near the old battlefield. Many people have reported ghostly encounters near the tunnel entrances. These reports include being touched by unseen forces. Many people have reported the smell of sulfur from cannons being fired. Both the British and French used cannons in the Battle of the Plains of Abraham.

Do the Dead Soldier On?

Soldiers are trained to never give up in battle. Ghost hunters say that is why people report so many ghostly encounters at former battlefields. The soldiers may not be able to give up the fight, even in death. During the American Civil War (1861-1865), the Battle of Gettysburg claimed the lives of about 7,000 Americans. One bloody battle of the Mexican-American War (1846-1848) happened in 1846 in San Pasqual, California. Witnesses have reported ghost sightings where these battles were fought. Reports include bloody ghost soldiers and ghostly figures of dead soldiers lying on the former battlefields.

Portland Tunnels

LOCATION: PORTLAND, OREGON

Portland, Oregon, is one of the largest cities in the Pacific Northwest. It may also be one of the most haunted cities in the United States. Many reported hauntings involve a series of tunnels running under the streets of downtown Portland. In the late 1800s, workers used the tunnels to move supplies between ships and local businesses. The tunnels also had an evil use known as shanghaiing. Criminals drugged customers in the local saloons and forced them through trapdoors into the tunnels. They sometimes took the victims to the nearby shipping ports and sold them as slaves to ship captains. Hundreds of people died in the tunnels after being kidnapped. Locals say the ghosts of these victims haunt the tunnels today.

shanghai—to kidnap and put someone aboard a ship by force

A woman named Nina is said to be one of the ghosts. According to legend, she was thrown down an elevator shaft at the Merchant Hotel. Today the hotel is a pizza shop. Nina's ghost is said to be a regular guest there. People say they've also seen her in the tunnels under the shop. She usually wears a long, black dress. Some people have reported smelling her perfume as she floated past them. Others say she tugged on their clothing.

One pizza shop worker reported a scary encounter with Nina. He said he heard a noise behind him. When he turned, he saw the ghostly form of a woman in black moving toward him. The ghost looked at him and floated toward the tunnel.

FACT

Most of the tunnels in Portland are now blocked off. But some are open for guided ghost tours.

A ghost hunter investigates the tunnels under downtown Portland.

The Mummy Museum

LOCATION: GUANAJUATO CITY, GUANAJUATO, MEXICO

In the late 1860s, people of Guanajuato, Mexico, paid a fee to have their dead relatives placed in the city cemetery. They had to continue to pay money to keep them there. If they could no longer pay, their relative was removed from the cemetery **crypts**. When cemetery workers removed bodies, they often found the remains in excellent condition. The dry **climate** and lack of air in the crypts naturally turned the bodies into **mummies**. For many years workers placed the mummified remains into a storage building. In the 1950s the city built the Guanajuato Mummy Museum to display the remains.

crypt—a chamber used as a grave

climate—the usual weather that occurs in a place

mummy—a body that has been preserved

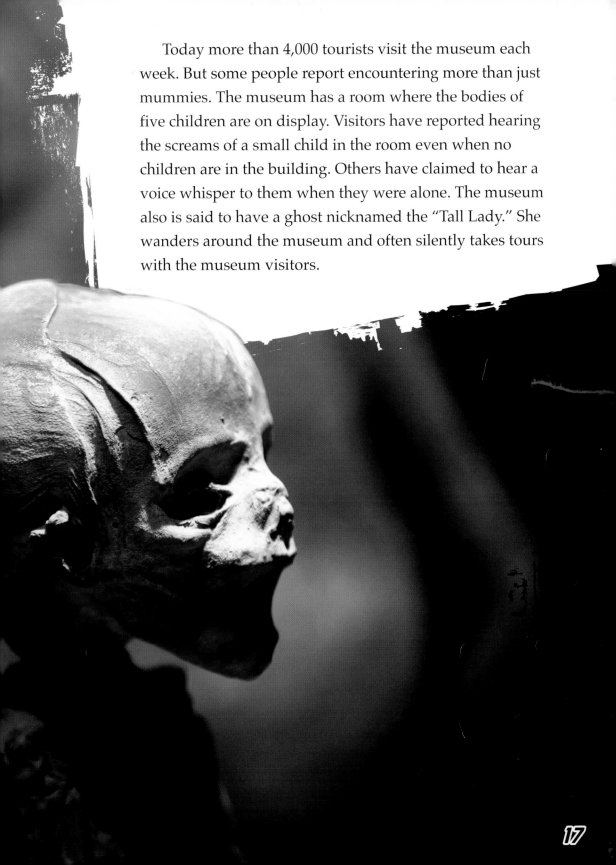

Today more than 4,000 tourists visit the museum each week. But some people report encountering more than just mummies. The museum has a room where the bodies of five children are on display. Visitors have reported hearing the screams of a small child in the room even when no children are in the building. Others have claimed to hear a voice whisper to them when they were alone. The museum also is said to have a ghost nicknamed the "Tall Lady." She wanders around the museum and often silently takes tours with the museum visitors.

Many islands of the Isles of Shoals have rocky coasts.

Isles of Shoals

LOCATION: NEAR THE
U.S. EASTERN COAST

Nine small islands off the coast of Maine and New Hampshire are the setting of several ghost stories. People have reported paranormal activity on the Isles of Shoals for hundreds of years. Some well-known pirates used the islands as stopping points. According to one legend, the famous pirate known as Blackbeard once left his wife behind on Lunging Island to guard his treasure. But he never returned, and she died. Visitors to the island have reported seeing her pale white ghost. The ghost is said to whisper, "He will return."

A shipwreck in 1813 on Smuttynose Island led to one of
its ghostly tales. The ship crashed into the island during a
winter storm. Fourteen Spanish soldiers plunged into the
icy waters of the Atlantic Ocean. According to local stories,
the wet, freezing men tried to crawl to the only house on
the island. Tragically, they didn't make it. When the island's
caretaker came out the next morning, he found their bodies
frozen in the snow. Two men almost made it to the house,
dying near or draped over the wall outside the property.

Today visitors to Smuttynose Island report chilling
encounters with the dead sailors. Witnesses say the ghostly
men wander the island as though they are searching for
their ship to return home. The ship itself is even said to
make ghostly appearances near Smuttynose.

Brockamour Manor

LOCATION: NIAGARA-ON-THE-LAKE, ONTARIO, CANADA

A cozy hotel called Brockamour Manor lies in the small town of Niagara-on-the-Lake in Ontario, Canada. But are its charming surroundings hiding a spooky secret?

Lady Sophia Shaw lived in the home that is now Brockamour in 1812. She was in love with Canadian Army General Isaac Brock. The two planned to marry when the War of 1812 ended. However, General Brock was killed in battle. Lady Sophia was heartbroken. She lived for a few more years in the home, but it's said she was never seen again in public. She locked herself away on the second floor. She died alone in the home in 1814. But she may have never left. For more than 200 years, witnesses have reported seeing her ghost at the Brockamour. She often appears on the second floor. Guests also claim to hear her uncontrollable crying late at night.

Locals also have reported seeing Lady Sophia's ghost throughout Niagara-on-the-Lake. They have spotted her walking along Queen Street crying. Locals have nicknamed the ghost "Sobbing Sophia."

FACT

A monument stands in Niagara-on-the-Lake to honor the life of General Brock. Witnesses have claimed to see the General's ghost in full military dress alongside his statue.

The St. Louis Ghost Train

LOCATION: ST. LOUIS, SASKATCHEWAN, CANADA

According to locals in St. Louis, Saskatchewan, Canada, a deadly train accident led to an eerie haunting north of town. According to the story, a conductor was working one night in the 1920s when a train ran over him. His head was cut off in the accident. Since then people have reported a ghostly light in the area. Witnesses say the unexplained light looks like the headlight of a train coming down the tracks. Locals call the light the "St. Louis Ghost Train" or the "St. Louis Light." The light is usually a white haze. Some reports say the light fades and grows brighter as it moves. Some people report seeing a red light with the white light. Legend says the red light is the lantern the headless conductor carries as he searches for his head. The city has removed the train tracks, yet the ghostly sightings continue.

Not everyone believes the lights are paranormal. Some skeptics say headlights reflecting from passing cars cause the strange light. Other people say swamp gas is responsible. Some people believe that as methane gas from swamps rises, it can mix with other gases. The mixture causes glowing lights.

FACT

In 2014 Canada made a postage stamp with a train on it to honor the famous legend of the St Louis Ghost Train. It was part of a series showing famous Canadian ghost stories.

El Hotel Meson de Jobito

LOCATION: ZACATECAS CITY, ZACATECAS, MEXICO

Some visitors to the popular El Hotel Meson de Jobito have left with a terrifying memory of their visit. Guests regularly report hearing the sound of children jumping and shouting when there are no children nearby. Some people report objects being moved mysteriously or feelings of being watched. Visitors report most of the paranormal activity at about 4:00 a.m.

Most reports involve unexplained noises. Guests have said they've been awakened by the sound of horses running through the halls. When workers investigate they can't find anything to explain the sound.

Ghost hunters often request to stay in room 107. People report the most paranormal activity there. The room is said to have belonged to a caretaker of the hotel named Don Jobito.

Alcatraz Prison

LOCATION: ALCATRAZ ISLAND, CALIFORNIA

Alcatraz Prison in San Francisco Bay, California, is a former federal prison. The U.S. government now operates it as a tourist attraction. Opened in 1934, it was once home to some of the most dangerous criminals in the United States. **Riots** and fights at Alcatraz left dozens of prisoners dead. Others died while trying to escape the island prison. Workers moved the last prisoner off of "The Rock" more than 50 years ago. However, visitors to the island say plenty of them stayed behind to haunt their former home.

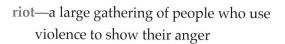

riot—a large gathering of people who use violence to show their anger

Violent Chicago gangster Al Capone is one of the most commonly reported Alcatraz ghosts. Capone passed time in the prison playing the banjo. Dozens of prison visitors have reported the sound of a banjo being played in his former cell. Tourists say they've felt bursts of cold air while approaching the cell. Unexplained temperature drops are said to be a sign that ghosts are nearby.

FACT

Police suspected Capone of many murders. But he was jailed for not paying taxes.

Al Capone's arrest record

K4805
(1939)

NO. 397-CAL
TERMINAL ISLAND
1-7-39

Scars and marks 5" sc. on left side of face

FBI NUMBER 214223

#214 223

CRIMINAL HISTORY

NAME	NUMBER	CITY OR INSTITUTION	DATE

More Than Prisoner Ghosts

It may not be just prisoners who haunt Alcatraz. Before European settlers arrived in North America, American Indians sometimes used the island to punish tribe members. They believed evil spirits lived on the island. Perhaps these spirits are responsible for some the island's paranormal events.

Cell Block D is said to be one of the most haunted areas of the prison. Prisoners were often sent to Block D after breaking prison rules. Prisoner Rufus McCain was often moved to cell 14D. Another prisoner killed McCain in 1940. A prisoner being held in the cell after McCain's death claimed that an unseen monster with red eyes was trying to kill him. Guards found the prisoner dead in the morning. He had been strangled. The murder was never solved. Some people believe the ghost of McCain killed him. Today visitors have reported that cell 14D is unusually cold. Visitors to Block D also often report hearing unexplained voices.

Haunted Locations of North America

1. Waverly Hills Sanatorium, Louisville, Kentucky

2. Fairmont Hotel, Vancouver, British Columbia, Canada

3. Island of the Dolls, Mexico City, Mexico

4. Plains of Abraham Battlefield, Quebec City, Quebec, Canada

5. Portland Tunnels, Portland, Oregon

6. The Mummy Museum, Guanajuato City, Guanajuato, Mexico

7. Isles of Shoals, off the coast of Maine and New Hampshire

8. Brockamour Manor, Niagara-on-the-Lake, Ontario, Canada

9. The St. Louis Ghost Train, St. Louis, Saskatchewan, Canada

10. El Hotel Meson de Jobito, Zacatecas City, Zacatecas, Mexico

11. Alcatraz Prison, San Francisco Bay, California

12. Myrtles Plantation, St. Francisville, Louisiana

13. Eastern State Penitentiary, Philadelphia, Pennsylvania

14. Silent Zone, Durango, Mexico

15. Sanatorio Duran, Provincia de Cartago, Costa Rica

16. Xunantunich Ruins, San Jose Succotz, Belize

17. Rose Hall, Montego Bay, Jamaica

GLOSSARY

climate (KLY-muht)—the usual weather that occurs in a place

crypt (KRIPT)—a chamber used as a grave

haunted (HAWN-ted)—having mysterious events happen often, possibly due to visits from ghosts

legend (LEJ-uhnd)—a story passed down through the years that may not be completely true

mummy (MUH-mee)—a body that has been preserved

paranormal (pair-uh-NOR-muhl)—having to do with an event that has no scientific explanation

possessed (puh-ZESD)—to be controlled by an evil spirit

riot (RYE-uht)—a large gathering of people who use violence to show their anger

shanghai (SHANG-hy)—to kidnap and put someone aboard a ship by force

skeptic (SKEP-tik)—a person who questions things that other people believe in

spirit (SPIHR-it)—the invisible part of a person that contains thoughts and feelings; some people believe the spirit leaves the body after death

tuberculosis (tu-BUR-kyoo-low-sis)—a disease caused by bacteria that causes fever, weight loss, and coughing; left untreated, tuberculosis can lead to death

READ MORE

Chandler, Matt. *Alcatraz.* You Choose: Haunted Places. North Mankato, Minn.: Capstone Press, 2017.

Niver, Heather Moore. *Are Ghosts Real?* I Want to Know. New York: Enslow Publishing, 2017.

Peterson, Megan Cooley. *Haunted Hotels Around the World.* It's Haunted! North Mankato, Minn.: Capstone Press, 2017.

INTERNET SITES

Use FactHound to find Internet sites related to this book.

Visit *www.facthound.com*

Just type in 9781543525953 and go.

Super-cool stuff!

Check out projects, games and lots more at
www.capstonekids.com

INDEX